Frances E Crompton

Master Bartlemy

The Thankful Heart

Frances E Crompton

Master Bartlemy
The Thankful Heart

ISBN/EAN: 9783744694186

Printed in Europe, USA, Canada, Australia, Japan

Cover: Foto ©Thomas Meinert / pixelio.de

More available books at **www.hansebooks.com**

"HE SAT DOWN ON ONE OF THE BENCHES UNDER THE LATTICES, AND MISS NANCY SAT BESIDE HIM." — *Page* 122.

Master Bartlemy

or

The Thankful Heart

by

FRANCES E. CROMPTON
Author of "Friday's Child"

NEW YORK
E. P. DUTTON AND COMPANY
31 West Twenty-third Street
1892

LIST OF ILLUSTRATIONS.

                                                  PAGE

"HE SAT DOWN ON ONE OF THE BENCHES UNDER THE LATTICES, AND MISS NANCY SAT BESIDE HIM" . . . . . *Frontispiece*

"SHE SAT UPRIGHT WITH ONE TOE ON THE FLOOR" 19

"HE WAS SPEAKING ALOUD" 41

"ARRAYED IN A SINGULAR COLLECTION OF GARMENTS" 91

"THERE WERE WORDS CUT IN THE STONE" 113

MASTER BARTLEMY;

OR,

THE THANKFUL HEART.

I.

IT was Miss Nancy's birthday. She was ten years old, and she had had a visitor of her own. And at Miss Nancy's age, to have a birthday is greatness; but to have a particular and personal visitor, real and grown up (not to say elderly), this is preferable to calling the king one's uncle. She had had birthday presents, but this may happen to any one, and had occurred before to Miss Nancy herself.

There was the Shetland pony from the squire, though to be sure this had been promised so long that it did not seem to have much real connection with the birthday, especially as you could not have it with you in the house; and there was the prayer-book from Aunt Norreys, with a red back and a silver clasp. Miss Nancy gratefully acknowledged that everybody had been very kind to her, from Mrs. Plummett, who had made the birthday cake with her own hands, down to poor Bettie the under housemaid, who had presented a humble offering in the shape of a purple silk pincushion, stuffed with bran to an inconceivable extent of tightness, and bearing in pin-heads the straggling device, "My Lov," which trifling error Miss Nancy, a delicate little person, both by nature and upbringing, would have blushed to observe, and the legend remained as unaltered as poor Betty's lov itself.

Even Trimmer, the stern, had given Miss Nancy a white and gold china poodle; and although the white and gold poodle may be an uncommon animal in real life, he looked charming in china, sitting tastefully on a ground of blue, which is well known to be the color of true affection. Miss Nancy had, with the friendly aid of a chair, set him up on the tall chimney-piece, from which elevation he stared fixedly and unmeaningly down upon her; and looking up at him in return, and thinking with remorse of all the pinafores she had torn, and all the shoes she had dirtied, and all the extra washings and brushings she had inconveniently required at irregular hours, Miss Nancy felt Trimmer's high-minded forgiveness to be more moving than language would fittingly express.

Arminel Anne Throgmorton was her name, — her Sunday name, as she was accustomed to think, having but rarely any other use for it than in the catechism of Sunday afternoon. Nancy was the name of dear daddy's giving and the name of every day, and Miss Throgmorton was commonly only Miss Nancy. She had, perhaps, at times wished that she had been endowed with a more ornamental and fashionable name; but as one grandmother had been Anne Norreys, and the other had been Arminel Throgmorton,

Miss Nancy quite saw that it could not have been avoided.

She had had a holiday in honor of her birthday, and Trimmer had even gone to the length of saying that she was going down to the village for an hour, and Miss Nancy might get out all her toys and take up the whole of the table if she liked. Not that Miss Nancy, though an only child, had any unmanageable number of toys; for she did not live in this present degenerate day of profusion in children's amusements, and the playthings grown old in the service of two or three generations were considered an ample provision for any one. The very best doll in all the collection was only a venerable and dangling lady, with a pink kid body, and a painted face, as ugly as might well be. Miss Nancy certainly valued her toys as toys *used* to be valued; but they did not lie very near her heart. A game with them generally took the rather forlorn form of laying them out in a solemn row, sitting by them till tea-time, and then silently replacing them in the cupboard. And even the pink kid lady, in her best yellow satin slip and real morocco shoes, had failed to satisfy Miss Nancy's soul to-day.

She knelt on the floor by the window-seat, so that she could rest her arms on the seat, and her chin on her hands, and look out at the prospect, which from this point of view did not embrace more than the upper branches of the great elm-trees, with the rooks swinging in their nodding tops in a high spring wind, for Miss Nancy's birthday fell early in the year. It was not an extensive prospect without, but it was more interesting to her than the one within, — the panelled walls and floor painted brown, the tiled fireplace and brass irons, the spindle-legged table with round leaves, the wooden-seated chairs, the cupboard where Miss Nancy's small possessions were kept, the dignified and indifferent gray cat on the hearth, and the tall, polished clock with the brass face, and brass balls at the corners, and the fingers that moved round in jerks, and works that groaned and wheezed for very age.

But now Miss Nancy had a visitor. To begin with, there was a knock at the door, and a man's footstep.

"You can come in, Bailey. It is only me," said Miss Nancy, well meaningly, however ungrammatically. The door opened, but Bailey seemed to stand still in a very unnatural manner, and Miss Nancy looked over her shoulder, to see no Bailey, but a living gentleman, rather an old gentleman, and quite a strange one. Miss Nancy scrambled to her feet with what would have been alarm if the old gentleman's appearance had not disarmed suspicion. He was smiling very cheerfully, and holding out his hand to her.

"I am quite well, thank you," said Miss Nancy at random, being for the moment thrown into some confusion.

"I am rejoiced to hear it," said the old gentleman. "You do not know me, do you? But I am the new rector."

"Trimmer is out," said Miss Nancy, doubtfully. "She has gone to the village. And Aunt Norreys has gone to St. Edmund's. And I do not know where daddy is."

"I have been walking with him," said the rector, "and now I have come to see you."

"Me?"

"Yes, I have come to see you," repeated the rector, with a gravity that Miss Nancy could not but consider flattering to a degree.

"Because of my birthday?" she said, feeling that at ten one begins to grow up.

"You see," said the rector, waiving the point, "I knew the squire many years ago, and now I should like to know his little daughter too."

Miss Nancy politely assented. She scarcely knew exactly what you ought to do when you have a visitor of your own, but, guided by a general strong sense of manners, she dragged one of the hardest and slimmest of chairs by its forelegs from the wall, and invited the rector to sit down, which he did, bowing his thanks, and drawing one out for her, — by the back, as more convenient to him than the low level of the legs. Miss Nancy infinitely preferred kneeling on the floor, with her arms on the seat; but this was, of course, not to be contemplated on such an occasion as the present, which demanded all the deportment of which a person was capable; and having smoothed down her pinafore, she sat upright with one toe on the floor, and the other dangling at some distance from it, waiting, in obedience to an ancient maxim which bade her speak when she was spoken to. She liked looking at the rector. He was what she called an old gentleman, for on the shadowy side of sixty one can no longer hope to be called anything but elderly; his hair was quite white, and he scorned to disguise that it had grown thin at the top years ago. He wore it longer than would now be strictly fashionable; it hung on each side of his face in fleecy locks, — like the apostles in the painted

"SHE SAT UPRIGHT WITH ONE TOE ON THE FLOOR." — *Page* 18.

windows in church, thought Miss Nancy. The rector's coat was in perfect harmony with his person, being old also, and far too long and ample in the skirt to have any pretensions to the mode. Miss Nancy liked him, nevertheless. He smiled at her, and he had a very pleasant smile.

"And what is your name, my little maid?" he asked.

"Arminel Anne Throgmorton," said Miss Nancy. "But daddy says Nancy."

"I thought it might have been something else," said the rector. "I thought it might have been — Margaret."

"Oh, no!" said Miss Nancy, earnestly. "Daddy would not like that. Once I said I liked Margaret better than Nancy, and he said 'Yes, but there was only one Margaret.'" For that had been the name of Miss Nancy's mother, and she was dead.

"Ah!" said the rector. "Ah, to be sure."

"But I like Nancy better than Arminel. Because when Aunt Norreys says Arminel, generally I have been naughty," admitted Miss Nancy, with regret. "I do not like Throgmorton very much. You cannot think what a hard word it is to write. I used to think it was a very hard word to spell. I suppose you know how to spell it?"

"Yes," replied the rector. "I used to write it long years ago, when I knew your father."

"And did you know him rather well?"

"I knew him very well — only, you see, we have not met for many, many years. And now he has asked me to come and live here."

"And shall you live here always?"

"I trust I shall, my little maid. I trust

that you and I may be friends as long as we live. How old are you to-day?"

"I am ten," replied Miss Nancy, with a ladylike endeavor not to show pride on that account.

"And I am more than six times ten. Do you think I shall be too old for you?"

"Oh, no! For if you are not too old for me, and I am not too little for you, we shall meet in the middle," said Miss Nancy, with much politeness, if with some obscurity. "There is not any one of great friends but daddy, and Aunt Norreys, and Trimmer, and a few of smaller ones."

"Then let us shake hands upon it," said the rector. Which Miss Nancy and he proceeded to do with mutual satisfaction, and the visit went on in the greatest harmony. Indeed, Miss Nancy was by this time beginning to entertain distinct hopes of the rector remaining to take tea with her, when she would be enabled to serve him with slices innumerable from Mrs. Plummett's birthday cake, and many, many cups of tea — in Miss Nancy's eyes the patent of honorable years; and this she thought would be a birthday feast indeed.

But, unfortunately, just at the moment when in fancy she was liberally assisting the delighted rector to cake, for the fifth time he rose to go.

"Must you really and truly?" said Miss Nancy, seeing the designed banquet melting away into thin air.

"Yes, I must go," said the rector. "My little maid, before I say good-by, let me offer you all I have to give." He was holding out his hand, and Miss Nancy thought it was to take hers; but he laid it on her head.

"God bless you, my little maid!" he said.

"And now," said the rector, at the door, "I have come to see you, and so you must come to see me."

"In fair turns," said Miss Nancy, nodding her head.

"Exactly," said the rector, and bowed his farewell.

"*Good*-by," said Miss Nancy, endeavoring to execute as perfect a courtesy as Aunt Norreys, — a sweet but delusive hope, to set a plain frock and pinafore against a full skirt of pearl-gray satin. And then the rector went, and Miss Nancy took him to the head of the stairs, returning to put the chairs in their places, with the feeling that after this anything might be expected to happen, and it would be as well to be prepared for it. The pink kid lady was also restored to the cupboard, for if she had been a little insufficient before, she had now become quite impossible.

"I have been having a visitor," announced Miss Nancy, with quiet and settled satisfaction when Trimmer came in. "He came to see me. Only me."

"Who was it?" demanded Trimmer, with cruel unbelief.

"He said he was the new rector, and I like him very much," said Miss Nancy. "He came to see me. Only me. And he said I must go and see him next, and I shall soon go."

But Trimmer, standing with her head in the cupboard, did not receive the full force of Miss Nancy's last observation.

II.

THE squire was a very shy man. The Throgmortons of Forest Morton had always been slow to come forward in any respect, and the squire was additionally characterized by that passive acquiescence which often distinguishes an old and almost worn-out family. There was no older name in the county, and none that had been longer established in one spot than Throgmorton of Forest Morton; but, at the same time, there was no old name less celebrated, and no house less interesting. The hall was almost as ugly as man could make it, having been rebuilt by the squire's grandfather in a style more to be remarked for solidity than beauty. A square house of dark red brick, a roof almost flat disguised by a heavy stone balustrade, and rows of windows of praiseworthy equality; in front, a paddock dotted with thorn-trees, and a straight drive between hurdles; on one side of the house, the gardens, on the other, the only remnant of the older Hall, the group of great elms where the rooks lived. The interior of the house was as plain, and heavy, and dull, for there had never been much romance, never much talent, in the family, — a family at no time more (old as it was) than a line of simple country squires, who had been born in Forest Morton, and had quietly lived there from one sleepy year to another, until they had as quietly died, and there been buried. The squire was a silent man from personal habit, and shy, with an hereditary shyness that nothing had ever been able to overcome. The habit of silence — if habit it were — had doubtless grown upon him, but it had been a habit even when his wife was alive. Aunt Norreys had said to her at times, "But, my dear Margaret, does John Throgmorton *never* talk to you?" And when she came to think of it, the squire's wife had not been able to say that he did; and yet there never could have been a more perfect understanding than that which existed between them.

The squire had married his second cousin, against the wishes of her guardian aunt, — for, properly speaking, Aunt Norreys was Miss Nancy's great-aunt. She used to say, "Why Margaret married him, *I* never could tell. If she must have married a relation at all, why could it not have been one of the Lester Norreys? Of course I have nothing at all to say against John Throgmorton, for he is really a very good sort of man, but it was quite incomprehensible, quite incomprehensible, my dear."

But Miss Margaret had married him, and the most incomprehensible part of all was that she had never rued it. Perhaps she had found more in John Throgmorton than did the world in general, perhaps she even had found in him all she had need to seek on earth. She had married him, and had come to the Hall to be the light of the house for a brief half-dozen years, — and then died. So the squire and Miss Nancy were left alone, to walk through the fields, and drive down the lanes, and sit in the square pew at church, in forlorn companionship, — the big, silent squire, with his brown cheeks and bushy beard, and his little daughter, with her mother's dark eyes and refined moulding, but too much like the squire in feature to have any pretensions to beauty. The squire and Miss Nancy had learnt at this time to be a great deal to each other, and indeed the latter had never felt that she required more company than dear daddy could give her; but her view was necessarily a limited one, and as usually happens in such cases, to add to a loss which nothing in this world could ever repair to him, the poor squire found himself plunged into innumerable difficulties with his household. So Aunt Norreys came to the rescue, and remained for compassion's sake, and tranquillity returned to the Hall. With Aunt Norreys and the dove of peace came Trimmer, neither maid nor companion, and a person whose severe aspect involuntarily, if unreasonably, suggested to the mind the old term, "waiting-woman." And Trimmer coming into contact with Miss Nancy's nursemaids found herself quite unable to agree with any one of them, and so differed materially with three in succession; at which point, for the sake of a quiet life, which Aunt Norreys loved above everything, she was permitted to ascend undisputed to the throne of authority, whence she governed Miss Nancy with a wholesome if rather severe rule.

The only remnant of the lawless old days spent with daddy consisted in an occasional escape from Trimmer, and a flying excursion in his company. The squire, as Aunt Norreys was fain to admit, was an easy man to live with, but he still preserved this reprehensible habit of coaxing Miss Nancy to go out with him on every possible occasion. No one could ever see that he took the least notice of her when he had succeeded; but if the squire and Miss Nancy were satisfied, that side of the question could concern no one else. The side which concerned Aunt Norreys and Trimmer took the form of those hurried retreats when the young lady had been caught in storms several miles from home, and, like Caroline in Miss Nancy's " Looking-Glass for the Mind," had been compelled to return home " in a most disastrous condition." But it was in vain that Trimmer appealed to Aunt Norreys, and Aunt Norreys remonstrated with the squire; he never by any chance entered into argument, and only turned a deaf ear upon them. Perhaps, indeed, there was something about little Miss Nancy's society which dimly recalled to the squire that of her dead mother; but whether it were so or not, he never said. Miss Nancy herself had a faint memory of her mother; she thought at times that home had seemed more when she was quite little than it had ever done since, and she believed that it was because mother was there. But she died, and it was to be supposed that it made all the difference. Miss Nancy could remember that day, when, very early in the morning, Mrs. Plummett came and took her out of bed, and carried her, wrapped in a shawl, to mother's room, Miss Nancy bewildered and half asleep, and Mrs. Plummett with an awed look on her comfortable face.

Dear daddy sat very near to the bed, and Miss Nancy sat on his knee, and mother held both their hands between her failing fingers, but did not speak, for she was speechless then, and only half conscious. So Miss Nancy was laid down for a moment to receive mother's strange, faint kiss, and then Mrs. Plummett carried her away; and Mrs. Throgmorton looked after her, and turned her dying eyes again to the squire.

And when day came, the nurse-maid said that mother was dead. But this Miss Nancy had not been able to fully comprehend, nor had she comprehended the strange silence and desolation of the days that followed. It was certainly not that she suffered then or afterwards an hour's neglect at the hands of any member of the household; it was rather from feeling a lack of something that she was sure she had had once, but had not then, and — alas, poor little Miss Nancy! — never would have again in all her life, that she dimly understood that she had sustained a great misfortune.

And Miss Nancy had also a vague belief that it was after this that dear daddy began to be even more silent than ever he had been before.

III.

"I AM far from complaining of Miss Nancy," was always Trimmer's opening when she *was* complaining of her. She even went so far sometimes as to say that she was a good child; but this, of course, behind her back, lest Miss Nancy should become uplifted. Miss Nancy *was* a good child; but the best of children will sometimes do the most unaccountable things, and who could have foreseen such an outbreak as the call she paid at the rectory? It could not have been called disobedience, for the simple reason that it would never have occurred to any one to forbid such an impossible thing.

Miss Nancy herself acted from a perhaps mistaken but deeply grave sense of propriety. The rector had said, " I have come to see you ; now you must come to see me," and Miss Nancy had said that she would, and a promise is a promise. She did not entirely like the thought of going alone, but she had waited a whole week, and neither daddy, nor Aunt Norreys, nor Trimmer showed any sign of going, and what was to be done?

So Miss Nancy went upstairs one afternoon with all the serious calm of perfect unconsciousness. She put on her boots (sitting down on the floor to achieve the act, as one does at ten years old) and washed her face and hands, and feeling that the occasion demanded an effort, laboriously buttoned herself into that very best bottle-green coat so peculiarly hated by her, which was therefore very conscientious behavior on Miss Nancy's part, when she might have chosen her old red cloak. Her best bonnet was out of reach, but she hoped the rector would excuse her everyday one. Then she went quietly and gravely downstairs, and set out to pay her call, far too much in earnest to remember that the drive was well commanded by Aunt Norreys' favorite window of the white panelled drawing-room.

Miss Nancy's heart beat fast as she opened the rectory gate, for she was by no means a fearless child; but courage is a higher quality than fearlessness, and she inherited from the squire a kind of silent endurance which could be made to serve as courage. A straight walk ran up to the house between wide flower-borders, with a hedge on either hand. There were daffodils nodding all the way up the borders, and in the orchard hedge was an almond-tree in bloom, pink against the blue sky. There in the walk stood the rector himself, with one hand under his coat-tails, and the other waving gently in the air. He was speaking aloud, and Miss Nancy thought at first that he must be talking to some one over the hedge; but as she came up the walk, she found that he was looking up at the almond-tree, and reciting with much earnest declamation of a quaint, deliberate, gone-by style —

"Plant, Lorde, in me, the tree of godly lyfe,
 Hedge me about with Thy strong fence of faith;
 If Thee it please, use eke Thy pruning-knife,
 Lest that, O Lorde! as a good gardiner saith —
 If suckers draw the sappe from bowes on hie,
 Perhaps in tyme the top of tree may die.
 Let, Lorde! this tree be set within Thy garden-wall
 Of Paradise, where grows no one ill sprig at all."

"HE WAS SPEAKING ALOUD." — *Page* 40.

Miss Nancy had been taught that it was rude to interrupt her elders, and she believed it would probably be also wicked to interrupt what sounded like a hymn, so she stood and waited until the rector had come to an end, and then advanced another shy step. The rector turned round and saw her.

"Dear me," he said, putting on his spectacles, "is this little Miss Nancy?"

"Yes, thank you," said Miss Nancy; "and I have come to call on you now." Miss Nancy, though a very simple child, was not a dull one, and there would have been a cruel awakening for her if the rector had even only smiled at that moment, as she stood looking up in his face. But the rector was almost as simple as Miss Nancy herself.

"You do me a great honor," he said, and taking off his hat, made such a slow, deep bow as was an admiration to behold. Miss Nancy bowed likewise, her coat pinning her too tightly to admit of any courtesy. "Will you come into my house and rest a little?" said the rector.

"I should like to stay in your garden, if you please," replied Miss Nancy, not feeling that she strictly required a rest.

"By all means," said the rector. "Let us go and look how the tulips are coming on."

"Yes, I should like that. I have not been in this garden before," said Miss Nancy, to whom the rector's predecessor had been rather a formidable personage. This rector was different from the first, and Miss Nancy slipped her hand into his from force of habit. The squire was quite accustomed to it, but possibly the rector was not. He did not speak for a moment, but stood looking down at Miss

Nancy, and when he did speak, it was to say something quite unexpected.

"God bless you, my little maid! you are very like your mother."

"No," said Miss Nancy, seriously; "Trimmer says I have not got any of her manners, and never shall have any of her looks. Then did you know her?"

"Yes, I knew her," said the rector.

"And didn't you love her?"

"I did, my little maid."

"Yes, everybody did, because she was so good. Trimmer says I never shall be like her, so it is no use. Did you know her quite well?"

They had reached the end of the walk before the rector answered. "She did not know me very well. I was much older than she was, you see."

"But I suppose it was a long time ago, when you were only a little old?" suggested Miss Nancy. "You didn't live here then, did you?"

"No, I came to be your father's tutor, when his father died, and he went to stay at Willmeadow, before he went to college."

"Tutor?" hazarded Miss Nancy.

"I gave him lessons," said the rector, smiling.

"Oh, *then* daddy must have been only a little boy. I believed he was quite big when he went to Willmeadow, to live with Aunt Norreys."

"He was quite big. He was grown up, and these were grown-up lessons, you understand."

"I see," said Miss Nancy, doubtfully; "but I did not know that grown-up people ever had any lessons."

"Yes, they have. They have them, indeed," said the rector, "even when they are quite old, only they generally learn those by themselves."

"Then you must have lived with Aunt Norreys, and mother, and daddy at Willmeadow. I know about that; sometimes Aunt Norreys tells me stories of it. And did you go on living there when daddy went away?"

"No, I went away too."

"With daddy?"

"No, I went alone; quite away. I, too, needed some lessons," said the rector.

"Mother came to be here after that. But she died, I think, a good many years ago," said Miss Nancy, vaguely. "Did you know that she died?"

"Yes," answered the rector, "I — knew — "

And at this very moment Trimmer came up the walk, avenging. There could, perhaps, be few things more mortifying to any lady than to be followed when she has set out to pay a call of some ceremony, to be caught just when the conversation begins to be easy, and to be dragged back home in the full light of day. In vain did the rector try to intercede for poor little Miss Nancy, in pity for her crimson cheeks; it *was* in vain; Trimmer was respectful, but obdurate, and drove the culprit away before her, as being in disgrace, and to be made to feel it. But Miss Nancy always did think that Trimmer might at least have waited until they had got outside the rectory gate before she shook her. Only slightly, it is true, but the ignominy was the same; and in mute anguish of mind Miss Nancy was conducted into the presence of Aunt Norreys, to make a full confession.

"Arminel," said Aunt Norreys, adjusting her gold glasses, "I am astonished, perfectly astonished. Immediately tell me the truth. Where have you been, and what have you been doing?"

"I have been to call at the rectory," said Miss Nancy, with bitter tears, but making searching efforts after strict truth. "The rector was in the garden, and he is very like an apostle."

"Arminel, what are you saying?"

"I mean, he has hair long like an apostle's, and I believe it is the Apostle John, but an old hat, a very old hat, older than daddy's," sobbed Miss Nancy. "I went to see him because he came to see me, for it *was* to see only me, whatever Trimmer says. We walked about the garden, and saw the things growing, and we talked a little."

"Arminel, what did you say to the rector?" demanded Aunt Norreys, with some natural dread of what might come next.

"I do not think I said anything at all naughty, I do not remember it," sobbed Miss Nancy. "We talked about daddy, and the rector said he knew mother a long time ago. But then Trimmer came. I think he hadn't minded that I went, I do think he hadn't. He said I did him a great honor."

"Arminel, do not be absurd," said Aunt Norreys.

At which point Miss Nancy fell into an unintelligible abyss of shame and grief, and was sent upstairs in disgrace; more as a preventive measure for the future, than as actual punishment for the past, but a consolation rather poor in itself, and not pointed out to Miss Nancy, nor perceived by her.

But the rector walked in the old rectory garden, and looked at the nodding daffodils, and the almond-tree, and the white clouds on the blue fields of heaven, and was aware of an eloquent sermon stealing into heart and mind. He thought he could still see little Miss Nancy walking beside him through the garden, and it was like some sweet old story of the spring that had been told to him long ago. For it is probable that the rector had had his own spring story in his day, and perhaps the memory of it came strongly back upon him, if he did walk about the garden with a hat even older than the squire's on his white head, and very tremendous spectacles absently riding high on his nose, and his hands under those most unfashionable coat-tails. And if one were curious enough to ponder the rector's simple, high-minded courtesy to the meanest woman in his parish, one might come to understand that there are some blessed spring stories, which may have no other happy ending than this,— that they leave a heart the better for their coming.

IV.

IN the course of some years' experience, Trimmer had more than once had occasion to remark that Miss Nancy's behavior, like that of many children, ran in grooves. When she conducted herself in a manner creditable to herself and her elders, she could be depended on for days, and even weeks; when she did otherwise, Trimmer was less disturbed in mind by the one deed committed, than by the immediate prospect of others to follow. Miss Nancy's next exploit was the more painful to all properly constituted minds, because it took place on Sunday. Nay, to confess the truth, it was actually in church.

It was a Sunday in what might have been either late spring or early summer. Miss Nancy always remembered that she wore a new Leghorn hat, and what Trimmer called a "lawn" frock with an embroidered hem, cool and spotless, and, like everything chosen for Miss Nancy by Aunt Norreys, plain, with that very dainty plainness which is fine in the extreme.

Miss Nancy walked to church with the squire through the hall fields. Aunt Norreys always drove, and every Sunday it was Miss Nancy's surest aim to have escaped, and have fairly set out with dear daddy, before the lumbering old family carriage came to the door. She had successfully evaded it to-day, she had safely set out with the squire, and she had plodded beside him through the hall fields to the churchyard gate, in the contented silence which always prevailed between them.

One went through the churchyard almost waist deep in meadow grass, under ash-trees so ancient and spreading that the little old church seemed half covered with the trees, and half sunk into the earth. The ivy had climbed triumphantly to the battlements, making of the tower one vast nest for hundreds upon hundreds of birds. They flew out, chattering and screaming at the sound of voices below, and fluttered round the tower in a cloud, —jackdaws, and starlings, and martins, to say nothing of the sparrows, who were everywhere, and chiefly perching in rows on the headstones. The porch was very small and sunken, the rafters low within, and the roof without so covered with ivy and traveller's-joy, that the doorway was like the mouth of a green cave.

You also went down a step into the porch, and down another into the church itself, in a manner agreeably contrary to your preconceived ideas, and which naturally caused Miss Nancy, a mooning child, as Trimmer truly said of her, to fall forward into obscurity with an unseemly noise nearly every Sunday of her life. It was dark and cold within, after the sunshine outside, the rafters were so low, and the flagged floor so sunken as to give a general impression of going down into the centre of the earth. The ivy had crept under the eaves into the church, hanging in corners like green banners; and the birds had followed the ivy, and fluttered here and there all service time. There were pigeons among the rafters (report said that Tummus Trowle, the sexton, was not quite guiltless of scattering corn on the floor for them during the week), and on drowsy Sunday afternoons the mice came out and played on the chancel floor, while the bats flitted overhead, like ghosts of long-dead mice.

But this was considered only proper to Forest Morton, the smallest and oldest church in the shire with its primitive tower of unhewn stone, and rude belfry lights, its low arches, and small windows deeply set in the massive walls. It might also have boasted of that marvellous old chancel wood-work, which had no counterpart in all the country-side. It was a standing admiration to Miss Nancy, a fanciful dream of figures, and leaves, and flowers, and sheaves of corn, and angels with outspread wings and palms in their hands.

Miss Nancy sat with the squire and

Aunt Norreys in the square Throgmorton pew, with her feet half a yard off the floor, owing to the shortness of her legs, and her head half a foot from the pew-back, owing to the width of her hat-brim. And Miss Nancy being rather small, and the sides of the pew rather high, the only thing she could see as she sat was the window opposite, a lattice of old green glass, deep in the wall. It stood open in summer, to Miss Nancy's great joy; for the sunlight came through it in a very enlivening manner, and she could see the apple-trees in Tummus Trowle's garden, and the ash-trees in the churchyard, and the white roses that flourished under the sunny window, and nodded friendly greetings, and even came inside when occasion offered.

Beneath the sunny window was an old friend of Miss Nancy's. She looked at him every Sunday, for he was always there, at rest on his worn stone tomb, being also stone himself, only he was such a dear old friend that she had almost lost sight of the circumstance. He lay in his ruff and gown, with his hands crossed very peacefully on his breast, and his gentle face looking upward. He was not a Throgmorton. Miss Nancy herself was of opinion that he was too beautiful to have been a Throgmorton, of whose looks as a race she could not think highly. Dear daddy was daddy, and as such forever to be admired; but from the dozen dull portraits at the Hall it could only have been concluded that the Throgmortons had been no more handsome than they had been famous.

All her life Miss Nancy had cherished a deep affection for this friend, looking at him when she could not understand the sermon (which was usually), and wondering how long he had been lying there so silently, and whether the roses peeped in, and nodded, and showered their petals on him, because they loved him. There were not many to think upon him, and the dust lay thick over his body, and in the few remaining letters of the rubbed inscription. " Here ly— Bartholom—." Tummus Trowle, when he swept out the church (a thing that, to do him justice, rarely occurred to him), called him Master Bartlemy and Miss Nancy too called him Master Bartlemy, and rather inclined to the belief that he had never had any other name.

Miss Nancy sat and looked at him, very upright, because of the brim of her hat, and very stiff, because her shoes dangled so far from the floor. The sunshine came in through the open window, and made a dancing pathway, which fell across Master Bartlemy's face; for Miss Nancy had observed that if there were any sunshine at all, it always lingered there. He lay and took his rest very quietly, and the buds of the white roses peeped in through the lattice, and nodded sleepily at him; and Miss Nancy too nodded sleepily, and would have fallen quite asleep if the envious Leghorn would have permitted it.

But then there came down a pigeon from the darkness of the rafters and settled on the old tomb, pluming himself on Master Bartlemy's breast, with movements so graceful and innocent that Miss Nancy held her breath for fear of disturbing him. And then he began to coo softly, opening his wings in the sunlight, and nestling against the crossed hands of him who lay there as if, Miss Nancy thought, Master Bartlemy might once have loved living creatures very dearly.

But Miss Nancy could not watch him to her satisfaction, not even by stretching herself out to be as thin and tall as possible. Interest outweighed every other consideration; if she stood on the seat she could see. Climbing was not exactly churchlike behavior, but Miss Nancy distinguished between a loud climb and a soft climb. The squire was leaning back in his corner meditating, with eyes half closed, and Aunt Norreys was leaning back in hers, perhaps meditating too, but with eyes quite closed. Miss Nancy knelt gently on the seat; Miss Nancy rose and stood upon it. The pew-sides were high, but in this commanding situation she was higher, and the Leghorn hat looked triumphantly round. The church was very quiet, the rector preaching, and at least a part of the congregation engaged in sleep. It was at this tranquil moment that the cushion must slide away on the seat; as Miss Nancy looked over the pew-sides it slipped farther and farther, and Miss Nancy came to the ground with a crash. Aunt Norreys, who had been (possibly) asleep, with difficulty suppressed a scream; while the squire, who had been honestly meditating, coughed as loudly as possible to cover the situation.

But nothing could disguise the fact that Miss Nancy lay face downwards on the floor, in her clean lawn frock, with the new Leghorn hat under the seat.

"Arminel!" whispered the scandalized Aunt Norreys. Even the squire himself said, "Hem."

"I have tumbled off the seat," returned Miss Nancy in a muffled voice, and somewhat superfluously, considering that this was obvious to the most casual observer.

"Immediately get up," desired Aunt Norreys. The squire more practically set Miss Nancy on her feet and returned to search for the Leghorn, while Miss Nancy stood wondering if there could be any spectacle more shocking than that of a little girl in church without a hat. The only thing that could be urged in favor of her conduct at this moment was that her despair was at least silent, for church was still church though one had disgraced one's self.

And then the squire, having angled under the seat with Aunt Norreys' parasol, landed the Leghorn, and set it on its repentant owner's head, but, a little unfortunately, back to front, in which condition Miss Nancy was then conducted out by Trimmer, the stern, who had suffered a shock that she could not have been expected to recover for the rest of the day.

"What you could have been doing is beyond my imagination, Miss Nancy," was her first observation, after walking half way home in a kind of stunned indignation.

"I only stood on the seat, Trimmer. I stood quite softly; I didn't know that I was going to fall so hard. I didn't mean to be wicked in church," said Miss Nancy, a prey to the keenest remorse. "I only wanted —"

"Well, what did you want, Miss Nancy?"

"I only wanted to look at one of the pigeons that was sitting on Master Bartlemy."

"On what, Miss Nancy?"

"On the gentleman who lies under the window — the stone one," explained the humbled Miss Nancy apologetically, turning her hat round.

"Miss Nancy," said Trimmer, with unabated severity, "I am ashamed of you."

"It sat so prettily, Trimmer," faltered Miss Nancy. "It sat on his fingers, and cooed to him, and Master Bartlemy seemed to be smiling. I was only looking a little, and then I fell off the seat."

"You cannot expect to do wrong, Miss Nancy, and not be punished for it," said Trimmer. Miss Nancy acquiesced in silence; but there was a further development of this point to be considered.

"Trimmer," she said, meekly, "do you think I shall be more punished?"

"Yes, Miss Nancy, I certainly do, for what else can you expect?" said Trimmer, uncompromisingly, and drove the debased Miss Nancy homewards before her.

V.

MISS NANCY sat in a window of the white panelled drawing-room, engaged in the pursuit of polite behavior. It was a wet day, and she had been sent to spend a sober afternoon under the eye of Aunt Norreys, the squire having evinced a dangerous inclination toward encouraging her to accompany him in a walk across the fields, a thing which Trimmer had reasonable grounds for guarding against.

Miss Nancy had finished her apportioned handkerchief hem for the day, and had been pursuing good manners for a full hour, without more diversion than she could find in herself, as was the antique fashion of her upbringing. Aunt Norreys could tell very agreeable tales when she was so inclined; but she was not always so inclined, and Miss Nancy did not dare to press the point. Not that she found it dull to be left to herself: it was a thing she was quite accustomed to; and looking now out at the rain falling softly in straight lines, and the wet lawn, and the stiff laurel walk, and the heavy peonies under the windows, and now in at the white panelled walls, and amber satin curtains, and spindle-legged chairs, and equally hideous and priceless dragon china in the cabinets, she had happily pursued one train of thought, until she had arrived at a point when an answer must positively be obtained.

"Aunt Norreys," said a gentle little voice from behind the long amber satin curtain.

"Well, my dear?" said Aunt Norreys, placidly.

"When I went out to ride with Giles this morning, Aunt Norreys, we came home by a new way; I suppose because it began to rain, and Giles wanted to hurry. It was quite new, I never went it before. We came along the St. Edmund's road at first; but that was not the new part, because I knew it as well as can be. But then we turned into the high pastures, and came behind the church."

"Was that all, my dear?" said Aunt Norreys, for Miss Nancy had stayed to consider it.

"It was nearly all the ride, because we soon came home after that. But it was not all I was thinking. I saw a place I have not seen before. I think it does not show from the village because of a good many trees. It was such a beautiful, beautiful place; a house all gray, not red, like ours. The trees of the garden were round it, I think," said Miss Nancy, wistfully. "I think it was prettier than our house. I should be rather glad if we had a roof that went up and down, and if our chimneys curled like those; and I wish, I do wish that we had a big pear-tree with boughs all flowers, and flowers, and flowers, over the end where the sun is. Don't you, Aunt Norreys?"

"Certainly not," said Aunt Norreys; "quite out of place, my dear."

"I rather do," said Miss Nancy. "Giles called it a Portingale. I said to him, 'What is this?' but Giles only said, 'This here is an 'ouse.'"

"Arminel," said Aunt Norreys, "I am astonished at you."

"He said so," urged Miss Nancy, a

little discouraged; "but I believe he meant, 'This is a *house*.' He said that it was only an old place where nobody lived. I said, whose was it, but he didn't know; and I said, why didn't somebody live there, but he didn't know that either. He said it was always like that, and he reckoned — I *mean*, he *thought* — it had always had been. And I said that I hadn't seen that place before, and what was its name? He said it was the Thankful Heart. I think it is such a very curious name for a house. I asked him what it meant, but he said he didn't know. Isn't it a curious name, Aunt Norreys? Don't you think so too?"

Aunt Norreys nodded her head gently, but gave Miss Nancy no open encouragement to pursue her inquiries.

"I wish I knew about it. I never saw a place like it before. I know names like the rectory, and Crabtree farm, and those things, but I don't know a name like the Thankful Heart. I asked Giles, but it was no use. So then we came home, because of the rain."

Aunt Norreys nodded more decidedly.

"But I know the way to it, if sometimes I might go, for I looked as much as I could. You go through the churchyard, past the window where the white roses are, and there is a gate in the wall, and some steps down from the yard; and they come into a lane, and you go up it until there is no more lane, but only gates. And after that, there is a way through a field, where there are more buttercups than anywhere else. And then," said Miss Nancy, leaning forward, with her dark eyes shining in her pale little face,—" and then you come to the Thankful Heart."

Aunt Norreys snored aloud.

So Miss Nancy stole out, and went upstairs to the brown parlor. Trimmer was not there, and she knelt down at the window-seat, and talked it over with the rooks in the elm-tree tops, having a sober friendship with them of life-long standing. They had the advantage of living so near the window-seat that they were very convenient as confidants, for Miss Nancy, however reserved, was occasionally compelled, like many other lonely children, to find some one or some thing to confide in.

But these steady old acquaintances, wisely and solemnly as they might caw to her, afforded no practical assistance in the present case, and Miss Nancy watched the rain and the rooks together, until Trimmer came in.

"Trimmer," began Miss Nancy at tea

time, "if you please, what does the Thankful Heart mean?"

"What thankful heart?" said Trimmer.

"I mean the house, near the church," said Miss Nancy.

"Oh, to be sure. Well, Miss Nancy, I suppose it is an old house, but I cannot say I have ever seen it."

"Yes, I know it is a house," said Miss Nancy; "but what does it *mean?*"

"Mean?" echoed Trimmer. "It means a house, Miss Nancy."

"But the thing is, why should it have that name?"

Trimmer preserved a discreet silence.

"Trimmer, do you know why?" ventured Miss Nancy.

"No, Miss Nancy, I do not."

"But it is such a curious, curious name. It makes me wonder so much. Don't you think it might mean something?"

"No, Miss Nancy, I cannot say that I do."

"But supposing that it did?" persisted Miss Nancy, resting her elbows on the table, and her chin on her hands.

"And supposing that it didn't," said Trimmer, tartly. "Miss Nancy, take your elbows off the table. That is what I am supposing."

"Yes," said Miss Nancy, obediently. "Trimmer, now I have taken my elbows off the table, could you tell me?"

"Tell you *what*, Miss Nancy?" said Trimmer, with some exasperation.

"About the Thankful Heart, Trimmer."

"I cannot tell you more than I have done, Miss Nancy. It is an old house, and no more, and no less."

"I don't mean that," persisted Miss Nancy. "I mean, *what* is it?"

"And haven't I just told you, Miss

Nancy?" demanded Trimmer, with a kind of exhausted patience.

"Yes," said Miss Nancy; "but you don't understand, Trimmer."

However, this sounded so exceedingly rude to an elder, that Miss Nancy blushed, and hastened to add, before Trimmer could reprove her, "I mean, I don't understand."

"No, Miss Nancy," said Trimmer, severely. "No, you do not."

"But I want to understand," said Miss Nancy. "Trimmer, don't you think you could make me?"

"You do not need to understand anything but your duties. To obey your elders, and tell the truth, and do your lessons, and mind your behavior, what more can you want, Miss Nancy?"

"I have tried to obey my elders all to-day, Trimmer, and I don't remember telling anything but the truth, and I have done my lessons, and minded my behavior a good deal, but *still* I want to understand and I don't."

"Then do all those same things more until you do," concluded Trimmer. Which was, though perhaps evasive on Trimmer's part, a saying deeper than she knew.

"Yes. Only still I want to know," said Miss Nancy, steadfastly. "But never mind, Trimmer, because of course it does not matter."

So Miss Nancy was led to bring the subject forward for the consideration of Giles, a person of an age unknown — though, as Miss Nancy believed, rather great — and of large attributes, in right of his self-arrogation.

"Giles," said Miss Nancy accordingly, upon the first opportunity, looking up from the modest level of the Shetland pony at the cross old face on the height of the squire's tremendous red horse,— "Giles, what kind of thoughts do you have about the Thankful Heart?"

"Ah!" said Giles, with an eye of untold wisdom, having never given much thought to the subject, but having a mind above admitting it. "Do you mean my thankful heart, or somebody else's?"

"I mean the one the house means," said Miss Nancy, somewhat obscurely,— "the old house near the church."

"Oh, ay; that same old place. And what about it, Miss Nancy?"

"I want to know what about it, Giles."

"Ay, well, Miss Nancy, I told you it had never been aught in my time but a gashly old place."

"Oh, *no*, Giles," said Miss Nancy seriously, dimly perceiving the term, whatever it might mean, to be a lowering one, "not at all gashly, *I* think. And you said it was an old place before. But I want to understand what a thankful heart is, exactly."

"Well, I reckon it is being thankfully minded," said Giles grudgingly, not being himself of that disposition.

"And what ought one to be thankful for?"

"For one's vittles, Miss Nancy."

"All of them?" inquired Miss Nancy, with a lingering hope that there might be a dispensation in favor of rice pudding, when partaken of for the fourth time in one week.

"Ay, I reckon so. And the clothes to one's back."

"Even if they are clothes you do not much like, Giles?" said Miss Nancy, faint-heartedly, with the new Leghorn hat stalking gloomily before her mind's eye, and the bottle-green coat that pinched round the neck.

"Ay, to be sure, for all one's clothes."

"And anything else, Giles?"

"For things mostly, Miss Nancy," said Giles, though it went to his heart to confess it.

"Then a thankful heart means, that you are to be thankful for everything you have, even for the things you do not like?"

"Well, I wouldn't say that," said Giles, inclined to back out at this view of the matter; "because I reckon a man couldn't be thankful for things as he *wasn't* thankful for."

"But it is generally rather rude to pick out things, you know. I think it does not seem nice only to be thankful for the things you *like* to be thankful for," said

Miss Nancy, deeply. "Don't you think so?"

But Giles did not think it by any means, and declined to allow that he did.

"It isn't having a thankful heart, after all, if you leave some of the things out," argued Miss Nancy.

On which Giles took refuge in a sudden access of majesty, and the discussion fell to the ground.

"I cannot quite say it," was Miss Nancy's conclusion, "but I think that it is really and truly *in* the thankful heart. If you have that, I believe you do feel thankful, always for everything."

VI.

"TRIMMER," remarked Miss Nancy, with studied affability, "I do know such a nice walk; you cannot think what a good one it is."

"Indeed, Miss Nancy," responded Trimmer, with but moderate warmth.

"You would like it very much, I feel sure that you would," pursued Miss Nancy. "Trimmer, when you want to go a new walk, will you tell me?"

"Yes, Miss Nancy, I will.

This was not encouraging; Miss Nancy was reduced to plain speaking. "I should like to go this walk very much. Might we go to-day?"

If poor Trimmer could have found any reasonable grounds for refusal, she would gladly have availed herself of them, for, like Aunt Norreys, she hated country walks, but Miss Nancy had to be taken somewhere.

"I begin to grow a little tired of the road to St. Edmunds'," said Miss Nancy. "I know it rather well, you see. And the road through the village, too."

"Miss Nancy," said Trimmer, determinedly, "my face is fixed against fields."

"The new walk is a lane!" cried Miss Nancy, triumphantly. "It is not fields, nor ditches, nor horses, nor cows. Trimmer, do you think we could go it?"

"I shall see when I get there," replied Trimmer, guardedly. "Miss Nancy, do not think that frock is clean enough to go out in, for it is not. And that makes three clean print frocks this week."

"I don't want to put another on, Trimmer," said Miss Nancy, in subdued accents; but, to propitiate the seat of government, made no further protest, and stood with exemplary patience to be dressed in that plain but spotless garment considered by Trimmer the only proper one for a young lady taking her walks abroad in the season of summer. Cleanliness came before godliness in Trimmer's requirements. Miss Nancy might accidentally be naughty now and then, but under no circumstances might she be dirty.

"This walk will begin like the village," announced Miss Nancy, when the expedition had set out. "You will think it is going to be through the village like the old one, but it is not. Presently you will see it."

Presently came just on the outskirts of

the village, when Miss Nancy opened the churchyard gate.

"Miss Nancy, where are you going now?" demanded Trimmer.

"It is a proper walk, quite proper," said Miss Nancy, stoutly, leading the way in much haste, lest Trimmer should change her mind, past the sunny window where the white roses peeped and nodded to Master Bartlemy, to a wicket in the churchyard wall, and down a flight of worn steps into a little lane, very narrow, and very deep.

"Trimmer, *this* is it," announced Miss Nancy.

Trimmer did not respond with enthusiasm.

"It looks very dirty, Miss Nancy," she said.

"No, it is only a very little dirty, Trimmer, and I do not mind it, I do not, indeed. And you do not know, Trimmer, for you cannot possibly know, how beautiful it is down there."

Trimmer turned down the new lane with the eye of one who has doubts. The churchyard wall was on one side, and on the other an overgrown hedge, so that the churchyard trees and the hawthorn bushes met overhead. This made the lane very attractive to a person of Miss Nancy's age; but a person of Trimmer's could not be blind to the mud in the deep ruts, and Trimmer picked her way with a very dissatisfied face.

"Isn't it beautiful?" breathed Miss Nancy. "But soon it will be *more!*"

"I hope so, Miss Nancy," said Trimmer plainly, "for I was just beginning to think that we would turn back."

"Oh, Trimmer! When it is just here — at least, only such a little further!"

"Well, Miss Nancy, I really do not see what you have come to look at," said Trimmer, but being by no means an unkind woman, though a strict one, she struggled on to Miss Nancy's goal. The lane ended in old iron gates, hung on stone pillars with great stone balls on their tops.

"And, oh, Trimmer, it is here!" said Miss Nancy.

"There is not much to see here, Miss Nancy," replied Trimmer; "I suppose it is only that old place you talked about."

Miss Nancy looked at her beseechingly. "And don't you like it? But, Trimmer, mayn't I stay a few minutes, and look?"

"Well, you may stay while I walk to the corner and back," said Trimmer.

Miss Nancy thanked her gratefully;

and Trimmer turned away, with the somewhat old reflection that there was no accounting for the fancies of children. What Miss Nancy could find to look at, she failed to see; and indeed exactly where the attraction did lie does not appear. Could we precisely define all those odd fascinations of our childhood, to which we still look back pleasantly, — if sometimes a little sadly? for alas, alas, there are no such dreams now-a-days!

Miss Nancy stood oblivious to all else, clasping the bars of the gates, with her face pressed to them, gazing in, with her very heart in her eyes, upon a meadow so yellow with buttercups that it was like a field of gold, upon a path leading through it to a low stone wall and another gateway, of which the gates were open, as if they had not been closed for a long, long time. Miss Nancy could see within. She saw a wide old courtyard paved with stone, filled with yellow sunlight, where the pigeons came down, and fluttered and strutted; she saw mellow walls, latticed windows, twisted chimneys, peaked roofs, overhanging gables, and apple and pear trees all pink and white with bloom. Behind, the rolling uplands where the sheep pastured, and the hanging birchwood falling down to the level meadows, and before, the field of the cloth of gold, where the buttercups grew, and in the midst, the house of the Thankful Heart.

"And don't you ever need to go inside the gates, Trimmer?" asked Miss Nancy, when she was finally torn from the spot.

"No, Miss Nancy, certainly not. How should I?"

Miss Nancy did not know, and pondered the matter with unspeakable longing all the way home. To visit the Thankful Heart had now become the chief aim of her existence; but she must needs bide her time in patience, for impatience had never in her life gained her anything.

But Patience is a sure horse, however slow, and, jogging steadily forward, carried Miss Nancy at last almost within reach of her desire. There came an evening when over dessert the squire said, "I shall be late for lunch to-morrow. Todd is coming from St. Edmunds' to go over the upland pastures with me. He is to meet me at eleven o'clock at the Thankful Heart."

He said it; and Miss Nancy heard it, and though pale with sudden rapture, still survived.

But good steed as Patience may be, she

"ARRAYED IN A SINGULAR COLLECTION OF GARMENTS."
— *Page* 93.

cannot avert the inevitable, and as poor Miss Nancy perceived from her window, the next morning was a wet one, and not a little wet, but sullenly pouring. She watched the weather with a failing heart all breakfast time, and well aware that in face of it any request preferred to Aunt Norreys could only meet with a most reasonable refusal, ended by trusting to her old expedient of escaping from Trimmer to join the squire at the last moment. But Miss Nancy was unskilful in strategy, and the enemy had overwhelming advantages, and presently surprised her in the act of flight, arrayed in a singular collection of such garments as lay at her command; an old hat of the squire's which could come to no further harm, her own red cloak, her strongest boots, and by way of great precautions, a cast-off pair of Trimmer's goloshes.

"Miss Nancy!" exclaimed the astounded Trimmer.

"I am just going out with daddy, Trimmer," faltered the guilty young lady.

"Oh, are you, Miss Nancy?" rejoined Trimmer grimly. "Now you will do nothing of the sort."

"Trimmer," said Miss Nancy, desperately, "I must go."

"Miss Nancy, take those things off immediately."

"Trimmer, I *will* go!"

"Miss *Arminel!*" said Trimmer in a fearful voice, for Miss Nancy's rebellious moments were so few and fleeting as to be an astonishment when they did come.

"I mean, Trimmer, mayn't I go? Oh, Trimmer, if I sit under the apron of the gig?"

"Miss Nancy, you know very well that

you may not. Your Aunt Norreys would not listen to it for a moment, and as for your papa, well, I hear him driving away now."

Which indeed he did; and Miss Nancy was left at the head of the stairs in such an agony of disappointment as we have all felt at her age, but happily not often afterwards; for although one's disappointments may be as keen, they lose at least the utter helplessness of those days.

"Miss Nancy, will you do as you are bidden?"

Trimmer's voice recalled her to herself, and to the fact that she really was left at home, and the day must be faced.

"I feel as if I should soon be naughty, I feel as if I — couldn't help — it!" Miss Nancy's voice died away wailfully.

"Miss Nancy, you know you never could have gone in this rain, so do not make a piece of work about it. Go and take those things off."

"I did so want to go, I *did* so want to go," stammered Miss Nancy incoherently, obeying more by instinct than anything else, and shuffling miserably after Trimmer, with the goloshes treading on each other's toes, and the squire's hat halfway down her face. "I wanted more than anything in the world. I thought I could go with daddy, if I was very good. Oh, Trimmer, and he was going to the Thankful Heart! And you have made him go without me. Oh, Trimmer, Trimmer, Trimmer!"

Trimmer was perforce deaf to this heartrending appeal; but she was a feeling person in her own way.

It is not indeed quite to be ascertained whether Trimmer had not herself undertaken the task, when one day she announced, "Miss Nancy, Mrs. Plummett's rheumatism being so bad that she cannot go out, I have to go for her to-morrow, to take some things to a sick woman. If you are good you may go with me. It is the shepherd's wife, who lives in the farmyard of the Thankful Heart."

But there certainly seem to be times when fate has nothing for us but buffets; which are doubtless salutary, but, like other salutary things, not to be taken without a gulp.

When Trimmer came to Miss Nancy's bedroom in the morning, she found her young lady standing on a chair before the looking-glass, the better to obtain a commanding view down her own throat. "I do not see it sore inside, but it feels as if it soon might be," Miss Nancy said, turning round a small, woe-begone face with wan cheeks and great, anxious eyes, and speaking in that croaking voice which always heralded a sore throat of that form to which she was much addicted, and which was the more to be dreaded because it was inherited from her mother.

"And Miss Nancy the picture of her this minute!" said Trimmer almost aloud. "And she was only ill three days, and it was her throat."

"Get back into bed at once, Miss Nancy," adjured Trimmer, "or I cannot tell how much sorer it may be. Now, you shall have your breakfast in bed, and we shall see how you feel after that."

"Do you think it may be gone by the time I have had my breakfast, Trimmer?"

"Well, we shall see," replied Trimmer, tucking Miss Nancy up in bed. "You must lie still now, and perhaps if you eat your breakfast, your throat may be better after it."

But alas, it was no better, even after Miss Nancy's very gallant attempt at her bread and milk, and the tears would trickle down her cheeks as she began to perceive that she must make up her mind to that only too familiar calamity which she dolorously called, "having a throat."

"I haven't brought it on myself, Trimmer, as you said I did before," she croaked piteously. "I haven't been in the fields with daddy all this week. And oh, Trimmer, Trimmer, I cannot go to the Thankful Heart again!"

Trimmer could find no immediate consolation for poor little Miss Nancy under this second grievous blow. It was but cold comfort when she said, "Well, Miss Nancy, if you cannot go, I will not, and someone else shall take the things," because Miss Nancy was fully aware that it was no disappointment at all to her.

"And you must not cry and fret," pursued Trimmer, "because you will only make yourself feverish. The better you behave now, the happier you will feel after it."

But it cost Miss Nancy a sharp struggle before she could say that she did not mind it now, at least, not so *much*. But she did achieve it in the end, having her little inheritance of that passive endurance that is often one of the dignified graces of an old house drawing near to its end. The squire came to see her, and Aunt Norreys sat with her for an hour, and so the morning passed, and Trimmer brought her dinner, which took the cheerful form of gruel; and, unfortunately, Miss Nancy hated gruel.

"Trimmer, need I?" she whispered, having by this time passed beyond the croaking stage.

"Yes, Miss Nancy," said Trimmer, hardening herself, "you certainly need, so take it like a good girl."

Miss Nancy looked at the gruel and fought with herself; but even in her small degree, she had not pondered the thankful heart in vain. She bent her head, and put her hands together.

"For what we are about to receive," she whispered courageously, wrestling with an enormous sob, "may the Lord make us truly thankful." And, seasoning her repast with some furtive and very salt tears, Miss Nancy attacked the gruel.

"And now you shall do nothing all afternoon but amuse yourself," said Trimmer; which sprightly promise she considered a very felicitous way of putting an enforced sojourn in bed, and so proceeded to invest Miss Nancy with a further dressing-gown, and to prop her up in bed, and bring her an armful of books. But while acknowledging Trimmer's kindness, Miss Nancy could scarcely fail to regard it as only a poor substitute for the Thankful Heart, and she looked at the books sadly.

For Miss Nancy's library was a small one, and the books were nearly all of a warning cast. The stories in the little red volumes of the "Children's Friend" were chiefly fearful narratives of the sudden deaths of children who flew into passions, or used bad language, or broke the Sabbath, and were apt to have a depressing effect on the mind, not to speak of the peculiar atmosphere of gloom that hung round the boy who asked to be put in his little coffin. And Miss Nancy never could see her way to holding such religious conversations with any of her relatives and friends as the standard of the "Children's Friend" seemed to demand — conversations such as the "Children" maintained with ease and fluency, and generally with the happiest results as to immediate conversion on the side of the elders.

In fact, Miss Nancy had never been able to find anything to do in the way of her duty, except the old round of obeying Aunt Norreys, and telling the truth, and minding her manners, and trying to be as tidy as Trimmer required, and learning her lessons.

Then there was "Kate, or the Punishment of Pride," and a very delightful book too, only unhappily Miss Nancy knew it almost by heart; and the same objection applied to Miss Hofland's tales. There was nothing left but the dear old "Looking-Glass for the Mind," and Miss Nancy turned over the leaves with languid fingers, and read of little Adolphus and Annabella's journey to market, and Alfred and Dorinda, and Anthony and Augustus or Rational Education preferable to Riches; and looked at John Berrick's quaint cuts of these stilted young persons in tall hats, and square coats, and long gowns.

But Miss Nancy's head ached, and her eyes ached also, and when Trimmer came again, the books were laid aside, and Miss Nancy was leaning back on her pillow, and, as she said, thinking a little about the Thankful Heart. For, like the stories in the dear, impossible, old "Looking-Glass," it, too, had pointed a moral, and read Miss Nancy a lesson that day. And little Miss Nancy, having concluded that this was one of those lessons spoken of by the rector, which we must learn alone, had addressed herself to the uphill task of learning it, with the silent patience that came of her gentle blood.

"And now, if you behave properly," said Trimmer, "I will tell you about what your mamma used to do at Willmeadow, until you fall asleep."

"I *am* behaving properly," gasped Miss Nancy in faint accents, with her hands pressed tightly over her lips, to keep the sobs back by main force. "I have tried to behave above everything you can think of, and I am not fretting, I am not, I am *not!*"

"No, Miss Nancy, I see that you are not;" said Trimmer handsomely, "and I will say that you have behaved like a young lady to-day."

Which high testimony filled up Miss Nancy's cup to the brim, it overflowed in scalding tears of various feelings.

"I can go on behaving," she said, with

the counterpane over her head, and a wet pad of handkerchief in each eye, " I can go on behaving till I fall asleep. But I cannot, I *cannot* be quite thankful enough yet."

VII.

VIRTUE was its own reward in the case of Miss Nancy's commendable behavior under the cruel disappointments she had sustained; or rather, it is to be hoped that it was its own reward, for she had nothing else. At least, she had nothing immediately, and one has to live in the immediate.

So she recovered, and the world went on as if she had not endured anything, as indeed it is very apt to do. For Miss Nancy had suffered. To have a sore throat was painful, but what was it to missing the Thankful Heart twice over? And in the meantime, the days were passing by, until Miss Nancy had almost fallen into a resigned way of believing that for some reason it was impossible for her ever to get thither.

But reparation has a fashion of coming to us from the most unexpected quarters. Nothing could have been further from Miss Nancy's thoughts on that midsummer afternoon, yet at the identical happy moment when, kneeling on the floor, she had engulfed herself in the lower half of the cupboard, to put away her lesson-books, — at that moment came Bailey to the door with the rector's compliments, and Aunt Norreys having accorded her permission, would Miss Nancy do him the honor to take a walk with him?

"Oh, Bailey!" cried Miss Nancy, emerging breathlessly, feet first, after a pause of stunned astonishment passed inside the cupboard, and knocking her head a most resounding bump against the shelf. "Oh, Bailey, she would, she would! Go and tell the rector; and run before he goes away, and say that she would!"

"There, Trimmer!" said Miss Nancy, in the height of her gratification.

"Very well, Miss Nancy, you will have to be made tidy," responded Trimmer.

Thus rudely brought down, Miss Nancy had leisure to remember her wounds, and, rather late, felt the back of her head. But Trimmer raked her from head to foot with a searching eye, as a preliminary measure, and as a following one, swept her away to her bedroom, whence she presently issued with a clean sun-bonnet, and the raw appearance of one who has just been washed and brushed with some severity.

"Now you may go, and mind your behavior," said Trimmer, who was a terrific dragon on the (now unfortunately out of date) subject of manners.

"Yes," said Miss Nancy, obediently, and minded it extremely hard all the way downstairs, and set off beside the rector with pride only tempered by a deep sense of the manners befitting the occasion.

"You see," said the rector, "as I was about to take my walk, it occurred to me that I should like company."

"I like being company very much," said Miss Nancy, seriously. "Generally I am daddy's, but I cannot be it always. And I do not enjoy being Trimmer's company so much, because she does not like anywhere dirty."

"I trust you will enjoy being my company," said the rector, with corresponding gravity; and they went out of the gates and down the long shady road to the village, side by side, the rector rather tall and Miss Nancy rather short, but still hand in hand, like dear friends. And then the rector opened the churchyard gate.

"Are we going through here?" said Miss Nancy, with a flush mounting in her cheeks. "I know a walk which goes this way. It goes down a lane."

"Exactly," said the rector.

"It is my dearest walk of all," said Miss Nancy.

"This is mine also," replied the rector.

Something rose up in Miss Nancy's throat then, and her heart beat thick and fast. If she were to be disappointed this time, she must disgrace herself, and that, too, before the rector. And they went on under the sunny window to the wicket in the churchyard wall, and up the forgotten little lane, to the gates of the Thankful Heart.

"Do we turn back now?" whispered Miss Nancy, flutteringly.

"No," replied the rector. "I generally go in, unless you do not like."

"I do like, I do like. I have wanted to go so much," said Miss Nancy, almost with a sob — "so extremely much!"

"Then I am rejoiced indeed," said the rector, and opened the heavy, old iron gates between the pillars with the stone balls upon them. They went through the buttercup meadow to the gateway in the wall, and into the courtyard, — a broad, stone-paved courtyard peacefully enclosed in its walls, with the mellow front of the old house on the fourth side; at one end, the pigeon-cote, with the pigeons cooing and nestling in the sun, and at the other a gray stone basin into which fell the

spring from the uplands. There were

"THERE WERE WORDS CUT IN THE STONE."

words cut in the stone over the basin; they said, "Give thanks." And the water tinkled into the basin, and rippled over its edge, and bubbled always the same words, "Give thanks, give thanks, give thanks!"

There was a door in the wall at each end of the courtyard, and the rector took Miss Nancy slowly round the old building. The farmyard was on the north side, empty save for the corner occupied by the shepherd of the flocks on the uplands. On the east side the meadow came unbroken to the walls of the house, and the sheep had come down from the high pastures, and through the fallen fence of the hanging birch-wood, to cluster under the windows; while overhead the nests of the swallows clustered also, and hung down one beneath another under the eaves. Miss Nancy thought that she would rather have tall dog-daisies, and waving meadow-grass, and a soft cluster of sheep close under her windows, and swallows chattering above it, than even elm-trees and rooks.

The garden lay on the south side, a wilderness of mossy apple-trees and overgrown bushes, and under the windows of the house a tangle of old herbs and flowers, with the great " Portingale " against the wall high overhead.

The rector and Miss Nancy rambled back into the sunny courtyard, and stood to look at the house, with its doorway so deep and wide that it was a room in itself, and its latticed windows in projecting bays, with gables overhead. There grew garlands of old pale-pink roses, so loose-blowing that they were more single than double, and under the windows great bushes of fuschia and Jew's-mallow. But Miss Nancy was looking chiefly at the doorway, and at the great oak beam over it, for there were words cut in it.

"In the Yeare of Our Lorde

. . . . .

Given unto God's Poore for ever,
In token of the Thankful Heart.
Amen."

"You cannot go inside, can you?" whispered Miss Nancy.

"We will go in, if you like," said the rector. "The shepherd's wife will bring the key. But I think you will find it a melancholy place, my little maid."

The door opened into the hall, with its walls panelled in oak, and its ceiling of oak cut into octagons by the beams, and its broad staircase with shallow steps. There were benches against the wall on either side, and in the middle was a black oak table, plain and massive; for this was the place where God's poor had been wont to dine together. But it was very chill, and bare, and empty, and Miss Nancy shivered.

What she had expected to find she did not know herself, but she *had* had expectations. Yet, alas! which of us in attaining his desire finds it to be entirely what he thought? Which of us, at last reaching up to success, does not sigh after all? It is doubtless well so; it may be a sense beyond our own control; it may even be that it comes from above, and would thither return, where there are neither strivings nor shortcomings.

But it was certain that from the moment of crossing the threshold Miss Nancy's dream began to be troubled. The rector led the way, and she crept after him, into one empty room after another, with lattices long closed, where the dawn looked in morning after morning, doors long open, where the sunset shone through into the passages evening after evening, and hearths long closed, where no light fell; down passages where a footfall echoed strangely; into rooms overhead, with gable windows looking out on the quiet meadows, and lattices of yellow light on the bare walls, and floors that creaked mournfully beneath the tread; and down the staircase that was still, and yet not silent, and into the hall again, from which the spirit of the old days had fled. And it was very chill, and bare, and empty; and Miss Nancy shivered eerily, and awoke from her dream.

The rector turned towards the door, but Miss Nancy did not beg even a few minutes' grace; she only followed very silently. She was thinking, in a desolate way, of a confused multitude of things, but principally she remembered that the sun-bonnet had been uncomfortably stiff, and the strings a degree too tight, when she set out on her walk, and she was beginning to wonder now whether she could bear it much longer. Poor little Miss Nancy! If her disappointments had been hard to bear, the awaking from her dream was far, far harder.

But that empty page, so unspeakably drearier than any written one, however crabbed, must be turned over with the others, when its time comes; only at ten years old one's philosophy cannot bear a very heavy strain, and the sight of the sleepy courtyard brought back the poor, foolish old dream so pitifully, that Miss Nancy felt that she must either untie the strings of her bonnet, or choke. Nothing seemed to care; the water rippled in the gray basin, and the pigeons fluttered round the dovecotes, and nestled in the yellow light, and the sheep bleated faintly on the uplands, and the larks sang high over the meadow.

And so Miss Nancy suddenly and inexplicably burst into bitter tears.

"What, Nancy?" said the astonished rector. "Have you hurt yourself? Are you tired? What is the matter?"

"I cannot bear it, I cannot bear it!" cried Miss Nancy. "I had meant so hard to be good, but I cannot bear it any more!"

"Bear what, my dear little maid?" said the rector, much concerned.

"I loved it so much, and I wanted to come to it more than anything. Oh, I did, I did!"

"And now you are disappointed in it?" said the rector, after a pause.

"I don't know," was all Miss Nancy could reply between the sobs.

"But I thought you understood that it was only an empty old house, Nancy?"

"I don't know. I didn't think it would

be like that," sobbed Miss Nancy. "And there is nobody there at all, and yet it says over the door that it was given to God's poor, — it says *for ever.*"

"Yes, my little maid," said the rector, slowly. "It *was* given to God's poor forever, — to the poor of Forest Morton parish. But that is the sad part that I told you of. The endowment failed long ago; I mean, Nancy, that there is no longer any money with which to support the old house."

"Then it is no use that the Thankful Heart was given, and it is all lost, and I am sorrier than ever."

"And yet, I would say, not lost," replied the rector, pacing the courtyard. "The spirit of the gift is more than the gift itself, my little maid, and that can never be lost, having passed once for all beyond us and our marring."

"But what is it?" said Miss Nancy, trying to suspend her sobs.

"I mean the deep thought of the heart, with which the gift was given, Nancy."

"I think I begin to know it," said Miss Nancy, "only I cannot say it. It means that nothing could ever take away that it was given once."

And the rector bent his head, and said, "In token of the Thankful Heart. Amen."

He sat down on one of the benches under the lattices, and Miss Nancy sat beside him, and wiped her eyes, with a vague sense, however little understood, of a quiet consolation. The water still rippled in the basin, and the larks sang above the buttercup meadow, but it seemed with another note, and there was a deeper rest in the peace of the Thankful Heart.

"Once upon a time, Nancy," said the

rector, "there was a man, an old man, who had almost come to the end of his days. He sat at his open window on a midsummer evening, — yes, it might have been such an evening as this. His work lay on the bench before him, but his tools were still, for he was dreaming; and he saw, as if they had been pictures, scenes that had been long ago.

"He saw a picture in a forest, the heart of a forest, where the deer and the squirrels lived, and it was cool, and green, and still. There stood two boys, about the same age, but alike in nothing else, for one was the young squire, and the other was a peasant boy, bareheaded, barefooted, and ragged. He stood looking down, with his hands behind his back, and the sunshine fell between the trees on both alike, — on the young squire and on the ragged peasant boy.

"'But show me what you were doing,' said the young squire.

"'I was cutting,' said the boy, in a low voice.

"'Yes, I saw, but show it to me.'

"The boy drew his hands from behind his back, slowly and unwillingly, and showed the piece of wood they held.

"The young squire cried out when he saw it, 'Have you done this? How did you do it?'

"'I have a knife of my own,' said the ragged boy, and he held it out proudly in his hand — poor boy, it was such a knife!

"'But you could not carve with a thing like that,' said the young squire.

"'My knife is a very good one,' replied the boy, with a glow on his brown cheeks. 'Give me my wood back. I can make it better than it is.'

"'I think it is beautiful already,' said

the young squire, simply. 'It is the Good Shepherd, is it not?'

"'What Shepherd?'

"'I mean the Good Shepherd Jesus.'

"'I do not know what you say. When my father was alive, he was a woodman under the old squire, and I had clothes, and my mother was there, and once I went to the church with her, a long time ago. I saw it then. A Man with a lamb on His shoulder.'"

"It would be like the picture in the window in this church, I suppose?" said Miss Nancy.

"Yes," replied the rector; "no doubt it would be like that. 'And you have remembered it so long?' said the young squire. 'How clever you must be! Now, I am not clever at all. If only you might learn reading, and writing, and Latin in my place! But I know what I shall do, I shall bring the priest here to look at your carving. If you will be here to-morrow, I will bring you a new knife.'

"The squire kept his word; he brought the knife in one hand, and dragged the priest with the other. The boy, too, was there; and the grave young priest took the carved figure in his hands, and looked at it, and was silent for a long time.

"'My boy,' he said at last, and he spoke in a very gentle voice,—'my boy, do you know the old carpenter who lives near the church?'

"'Him who buys the squire's trees, and makes things of wood?' said the boy.

"'Yes, the old carpenter. You shall go to him, and learn his craft; for God who gave you those hands to work with never meant you to be only a vagabond on the face of the earth; surely He designed you to be something better.' . . .

"The old man saw another picture. The ragged boy presented himself one morning at the old carpenter's door, with his ragged tunic, and bare head and feet; if it had cost him anything to leave the forest and his freedom, he never told it.

"But now began a new life for him. He learnt more quickly than the old carpenter could teach; it seemed as if he knew the natures of the dead woods by instinct, as he had known the living trees in the forest.

"'But now you must put aside those carved toys that are always in your fingers,' grumbled the old carpenter; 'you will never make a good workman if you waste your time over them.' But he was very kind to the boy nevertheless, and he learned to love him very dearly, for his own children were all dead. They went to church together, and the boy sat and looked up with his deep bright eyes at the beams of the roof, and at the pillars, and arches, and the pale pictures in the windows.

"The young squire was his fast friend, until he went away from the village; but the priest did not go away, and it was he who taught him to read and write, and taught him the catechism and the Psalms, and indeed taught him many things; but he did not need to teach him the knowledge that comes of the seeing eye, and the reverence that comes of a believing heart, for he had learnt those things in the school of the forest, and his teacher had been none other than God himself. . . .

"The old man saw another picture. The young squire had come home; they said he was to be married. He came to see the boy, for he had never forgotten him;

and he walked with the priest through the meadows. It was evening, and the old carpenter sat at his door.

"'He has finished his work,' he said. "He has gone up to the little room in the gable, for he is often there, but why, I cannot tell. Let us go up and find him.'

"They went upstairs to the little room; they pushed open the door and went in. The boy was a boy no longer, but a tall young man; he was standing up to stretch his arms, and the light shone full on his face, the same face as of old, with marvellous deep eyes, and earnest lips which nevertheless smiled. His chisel was in his hand, and his work before him, a panel of English oak, traced over with a wonderful fret of leaves and flowers, a part carved in relief, and the rest still drawn in charcoal. His tools lay on a stool beside him, very few and simple, for the power was in his own hands, not in the tools they held; the wall before him was covered with his designs, drawn in charcoal, after his only teaching, which he had found in the school of the forest. But there was love, and patience, and reverence in every line, drawn again and again, and yet again, until the artist hand could execute what the faithful eye could see.

"'It is wonderful!' said the priest.

"'It is most beautiful!' said the squire, for he thought that the priest spoke of the work. 'You were born a great carver, and now you shall go to London and work there.'

"'Yes, you shall go to London,' said the priest.

"But the carver looked at the old carpenter, and his eyes fell. And there was a long silence, until at last the old man said, in a broken voice, 'Yes, you shall go. You shall go.' . . .

"The old man saw another picture. The young carver was setting out from the door, with his little bundle over his shoulder. The old carpenter blessed him, and let him go, without a word to stay him; but whenever the young man turned round, the old one was still looking after him, until at last he went over the brow of the hill. And then the old carpenter turned away sadly. 'How could I stay him? He, too, is gone,' he said; and he went into his house and shut the door.

"But after it was dusk in the evening, there came a gentle knocking at the door, and when he opened it, the carver stood upon the threshold.

"'Master, I have returned,' he said.

"'To stay yet another night, dear son?' said the old man, trembling.

"'Even to the end,' said he.

"'My son?' said the old man, trembling more.

"'I am resolved,' he answered, and his face against the sky was very pale.

"'God reward you, my son!' replied the old man, weeping, 'seeing that I never can.'

"He only bowed his head, and said within himself, 'Nay rather, God give me grace still to thank him.'

"He said to the squire, 'He has given me so much, that I may surely give back to him, even if it be only giving up.'

"But that, my little maid, is a hard thing to give, — yes, the hardest of all. And doubtless the priest knew it, for he only said, 'It is by the grace of God.'"

"I love him for coming back," said Miss Nancy, sadly; "but I wish he might have gone to be a great carver. It wasn't a wrong thing to want, was it?"

"No, it was not wrong, my little maid. It was good to desire it, but to so give it up was far, far better. And that picture stayed a long time before the old man's eyes, and he dreamed over it. He saw the carver go up to the room in the gable, and look at his work, and turn its face to the wall, and go out again. He saw him toiling day by day in the workroom below, for now it was he who supported the old carpenter; and he thought of him always there in the same place, until ten long years were past. Until one evening the old carpenter said, 'Now you shall soon have your release. Come and let me bless you, good son.' And in that night the old carpenter died. . . .

"The old man saw another picture. Now the carver was setting out at last to seek his fortune in earnest. And the old man saw that the priest and the squire walked with him to the highway, and bade him farewell, and stood to watch him until he had gone over the brow of the hill, but he did not hear what they said. 'God bless him!' said the squire. 'If he had gone ten years ago, he might have been a great man.'

"'He will yet be a great man,' said the priest, and mused. 'Perchance in God's sight he is already great.'

"And they went home, and thought of him when the evening fell. But sunrise came, and sunset, and moon followed moon, and summer and winter went by, and so the years passed.

"But the old man saw the carver go out into the world to seek his fortune, and saw him find it, for it was to work with all his heart, as a man should work; and he went here and there, and many things befell him."

"And did he come to be a great carver?" said Miss Nancy.

"He did, my little maid, though success, as we account it, only came to him late in life; and men said he had begun too late. Not so; he had waited for God's time with a noble patience. Did he value the success when it did come, as he would have done when he was young? Ah, that I cannot tell; but in his day he was a carver, as some say, never equalled, and as all say, never surpassed, though perhaps it was only after his death that men came fully to this understanding. And at last he would stay no longer to work in cities, for he had through all this latter part of his life an exceeding great longing to see the green forest once more, and, if it might be, to lie down under the shadow of the church."

"He must have grown old, I suppose?"

said Miss Nancy, wistfully. "But generally in tales the people who seek their fortune find it before they grow old."

"Yes, he had grown old," said the rector. "That is, as we count years. But one is fashioned after this manner, and another after that, and thanks be to the good Fashioner of all, there are some who never grow old. And so at last the carver set his face homeward along the old highway, and began to bring his adventures to an end. . . .

"The old man saw another picture. He saw the carver walking with the old priest and the squire through the long grass of the meadows to the house by the church. They found only a habitation for owls and bats; but the carver bought the house and rebuilt it. He went up to the room in the gable, and found the half-finished panel, gray with dust and cobwebs, still turned with its face to the wall, as he had left it so many years ago. He said, 'This was begun at the entering of my life, for the love of the beautiful earth beneath; it shall be finished at the close, for the love of the fairer heaven above.'

"And so he began the famous twelve apostle panels, as all men said, his best work, and, as he said, his dearest. It was also his last; for the time began to draw near when he should bring his steadfast life to a good ending. . . .

"And so the old carver awoke from his dreams, and thought upon his life, and gave God thanks for it.

"A shadow fell through the doorway. It was the aged priest and the squire, who came to sit with him, as they so often did in the evening.

"'Is the work finished?' said the priest.

"'Almost,' he answered; 'this evening it will be finished.'

"And so the three old men sat at the open window, and talked of what had been in the old time, and of what might be when time should be no more. And suddenly the carver raised his head from his work, and said, 'I go first. Last night I dreamed of a fair stream.'

"And they were silent, knowing that to dream of a fair stream is a sign of coming death.

"The priest said, 'Was that a happy dream?'

"The carver answered, 'I walked upon the brink of the stream, a stream all peaceful, flowing full between green reeds. And once more I was a child again; and I beheld the Good Shepherd, even as I thought of Him when I was a child, coming through the lilies in the grass, with little children, as it were lambs, gathered about Him. He said, "Thou hast learned a while in My school. My child, now see the end of thy learning," and I awoke. It was a blessed dream.'

"'Only may this work be first finished,' said the priest.

"'It is finished even now,' he said; and he laid down his tools for the last time.

"It lay complete before them, twelve panels of oak, wrought as men had never seen the like in all the countryside, for that great master had spent upon them all the gathered skill, and patience, and love of a lifetime. Upon each panel the figure of a holy apostle; and round about a fret of leaves and flowers, as it were for beauty; and at the foot of each panel a border of corn, for service; and above each an angel's head with wings, for praise, and in his hands a palm for victory; and humbly wrought in a hidden corner the sign of the carver's own hand, a heart, as it were for thanksgiving.

"'It is finished,' he said. 'I have not achieved the half I had designed to do; but He who has deigned to have need of my work, will also call me there, where, having here learned awhile, I may in fuller knowledge make an end.'

"And he looked up and smiled.

"They said it was granted to him then to see a vision. It might have been that the eyes which had not failed to discern the beauty of God as it is on earth were opened then to behold it as it is where we all would be at the last; I cannot tell, only after a moment he covered his face with his hands.

"'My God, I thank thee,' he said, and laid his head down upon his work, and died." . . .

"I think it is a little sorrowful," said Miss Nancy; "but perhaps it is more happier than more sorrowfuller. And is that quite all?"

"There is little more," said the rector.

"The old priest who loved him so much wrote about his life; and he said that he and the squire knew not whether they had more grief or joy for his end."

"And does the story tell what they did after it?"

"A little more," said the rector again.

"He had prayed them to let him lie very near the church, for he had loved that little church in the shadow of the green forest most of any place on earth. So they buried him there, not without the walls, but within, for the priest said, he was the best of all men he ever knew;

and the squire set a beautiful figure of the carver there upon the tomb in the church, that it should be well seen how he had worshipped God in life, and now worshipped him yet more worthily after death."

"And is that quite, quite all?"

"Almost, my little maid," answered the rector, slowly. "He had disposed of all that he had, as men dispose before they die; and they read what he had written. He gave to his friends, the priest and the squire, what keepsakes they might choose, in memory of the love he bore them. . . . He gave the twelve apostle panels, his last and dearest work, to the church he had loved so well. . . . He gave his house and his goods to God's poor forever. . . . And as he humbly prayed God to receive, though so unworthy of his merciful receiving, all that now was left to him, — his thankful heart."

"Yes, I know," whispered Miss Nancy, — "I know. It was Master Bartlemy."

VIII.

IT was a hard winter, the hardest in the memory of Grandfy Purcell, the oldest inhabitant of Forest Morton parish. The frost had set in before Christmas, and though the New Year had long since come, it still bit the harder, in defiance of all old saws.

The world and the weather both were gloomy faces for Miss Nancy. Aunt Norreys had gone to pay a solemn visit, "to the Lester Norreys, my dear," and had insisted upon the reluctant squire going also. A regency had been formed at the hall, with Mrs. Plummett at the head of the household, Trimmer being always at the head of the brown parlor; and Miss Nancy had been put upon her honor as regarded her behavior.

She looked upon this separation from daddy in a very serious light, and since his departure she had conducted herself in a correspondingly serious manner; but life must be lived even after partings, and Miss Nancy had never forgotten that her behavior was to be based on the grounds of honor. But the days passed very slowly, and Trimmer did not feel sure that she did not flag more as time went on, instead of less.

It was indeed a hard winter. All afternoon from the window of the brown parlor Miss Nancy watched the snow falling, until there was a white mantle over the Hall fields, and a deep drift blown under the elm-trees. The rooks, with melancholy cawings, had early retired to rest, before the red sun had set, and the moon had risen over the hawthorn copse; at which point Trimmer had insisted on the curtains being drawn, and Miss Nancy coming to tea.

Miss Nancy and Trimmer sat at tea, one at each end of the spindle-legged table with round leaves, Trimmer mellowing over her second cup of tea, and Miss Nancy plodding through her bread and butter with perhaps more conscientiousness than enjoyment, very good, as she had been throughout the regency, but also very quiet.

"Why, Miss Nancy, you have not finished your tea yet," said Trimmer looking up at last.

"I think I do not want this tea much," said Miss Nancy, laying down a horned moon of bread and butter. "I feel very sorrowful with dear daddy being away."

"Well, he will soon be home now. Finish your tea, Miss Nancy."

Miss Nancy picked up her crescent sadly, regarded it with but small interest, and took a slow bite.

"And make haste," said Trimmer; "see what a long time you have been."

"I think I do not want it at all, Trimmer," said Miss Nancy, laying it down again.

"Oh, the idea!" said Trimmer, simulating an incredulous astonishment, Miss Nancy's appetite being a small thing at the best, and a diminution of it a point to be elaborately ignored. "Miss Nancy, eat it up directly!"

Thus adjured, Miss Nancy at last disposed of it; and grace having been said, Trimmer betook herself to her knitting, and Miss Nancy to that one of the stern wooden chairs which seemed the most yielding, and established herself at the spindle-legged table with "Original Tales of a Moral Tendency for Young Ladies and Gentlemen." The firelight lit up the formal old room, and cast a friendly glance upon the brown walls, and touched the polished chairs here and there, and warmed the brass balls of the clock into a silver glow. The clock wheezed and the fire crackled, the gray cat snored on the hearth and the wind moaned in the elms outside, but Miss Nancy was very still. In point of fact, when Trimmer looked at her, her head was laid down on the tales of moral tendency, and her eyes were closed.

"Miss Nancy, what are you doing to fall asleep over your reading?" said Trimmer. "Bed is the place for going to sleep."

"I want to go to sleep here — just here," said Miss Nancy, with feeble dignity, her eyes opening and closing again.

"Oh, but that is quite impossible," said Trimmer, briskly. "You will have a headache, Miss Nancy, so sit up."

Miss Nancy raised her head, and rested it on her hand; the firelight fell on her face, and Trimmer looked at it over her knitting. "Miss Nancy," she said presently, laying down her work, "do you think you would like to go to bed?"

Miss Nancy nodded wearily.

"Because you may, if you like," said Trimmer, without a sign of surprise at Miss Nancy's ready assent; "you may come with me now."

"Yes," said Miss Nancy, but did not move.

So Trimmer carried her. Miss Nancy made no resistance; her head fell down on Trimmer's shoulder as if it were so heavy that she could hold it up no longer. Nor could she hold it up even while she was being undressed; it seemed to her as if she fell asleep three distinct times, and had three distinct long sleeps during that operation. But she was put to bed at last, and tucked in; and Trimmer sat down behind the curtain, with a candle and her knitting, just as if, Miss Nancy thought, she were having a sore throat.

And then she fell asleep, and slept very heavily; and when she woke, it was very early in the morning, and she was having a sore throat in good earnest.

"Trimmer, it is sore, very, very sore," she whispered.

"Yes, Miss Nancy, I thought it might be going to be," said Trimmer, from the hearth, and it did not occur to Miss Nancy to wonder what she was doing there at that time of day, or rather night.

"I never felt it like this before. Oh, Trimmer, do you think it will be worse?"

"Don't talk, Miss Nancy, and I will get you something to drink."

"But, oh, Trimmer," said Miss Nancy, clasping her hot fingers, "suppose it should grow worse and worse while daddy is away."

"I think it will be all right, Miss Nancy," said Trimmer, steadily. "I am seeing after you. And your papa and your Aunt Norreys will be coming home in a few days."

Then after an hour or two, when it was still quite early in the morning, the old doctor came from St. Edmunds' to look at Miss Nancy; and she wondered confusedly if he had come just as it were by chance, or whether Trimmer had sent for him, in which case Miss Nancy believed that she must be quite ill.

After he was gone she lay and tossed from side to side, and fell asleep again, and dozed fitfully all day, and between the dozes started up with her eyes bright and her hands burning.

"Never mind it, Miss Nancy, my dear," said Trimmer, sitting always by the bed as if she had never moved away. "It is only a bad dream you have been having."

"I have been so afraid," said Miss Nancy, hoarsely. "Oh, Trimmer, has daddy come home?"

"Not yet, Miss Nancy; I am expecting him soon," said Trimmer, with as much composure as if she and Mrs. Plummett had not sent an urgent message to the squire and Aunt Norreys as soon as the doctor had been.

"I wish he would come!" gasped Miss Nancy.

"And, oh, my dear, so do I!" thought Trimmer.

Miss Nancy dozed again, and gradually evening drew on; she believed that the doctor came then, but she did not feel sure of it. She also believed that he came again some time after she had watched the first pale streaks of the gray morning appearing behind the elms, after that long, unquiet fevered night; but she could not feel sure of that either, for her mind was in a very hazy condition. The morning dragged itself by, and Miss Nancy lay and slept, and moaned a little in her sleep, and before noon Trimmer and Mrs. Plummett had despatched a second messenger; for by this time they had come to such a frame of mind that they would almost have forfeited everything they had in the world to have the squire and Aunt Norreys at home.

But Miss Nancy lay and knew nothing of all this uneasiness on her behalf. She asked for daddy many times, in a hoarse, gasping whisper; Trimmer always told her that he was coming. But the afternoon passed, and the evening fell, and darkness came, and it was not until far into the night that Mrs. Plummett, straining her ears miserably at the head of the stairs, burst into tears of thankfulness, as Bailey, stiff with waiting, opened the door to see lights twinkling through the bare thorn-trees, as the carriage dashed up the drive. But this haste made no difference at all to Miss Nancy, for when the squire and Aunt Norreys came, she did not know them.

For Miss Nancy was having dreams, a great many of them. It seemed to her to be one long night, the longest she had ever known. Sometimes she thought she was awake, and was very ill; but this was a fancy that came and went. The world floated hither and thither, and left Miss Nancy drifting forlornly by herself; but one thing always remained, and that was a sore throat. How long it was dark round her bed she did not know, but she dreamed some very curious things. She dreamed not only about the old doctor from St. Edmunds', but about the other doctor from Carchester, and then about a gentleman whom she did not know.

She dreamed fitfully about the old friends when her sleep was not so deep that she was unconscious of anything. Trimmer seemed to be always there, and her face was quite white, all but a line under her eyes, and that was purple; and Miss Nancy dimly wondered at it, not knowing that the nursing of little Miss Throgmorton would be told in honor of Trimmer the stern as long as she lived. She dreamed of Aunt Norreys being by the bed; and once when she sat there, Miss Nancy was almost sure that she was crying, and she wondered at that too, not knowing that the great London doctor believed that little Miss Throgmorton was dying.

Daddy was often, often there, standing at the foot of the bed, silently, with mournful eyes; and this was the most troubled dream of all. And when he was not there, he was sitting, though Miss Nancy did not know it, in his justice-room downstairs, silent and alone, hour after hour, except when the rector came to be with him.

Nor did Miss Nancy know that in those hours of her night when the great London doctor believed that she was dying, the squire and the rector sat side by side in the room below, looking dumbly at a pitiful scrawl on the table before them, written on a leaf of a copy-book, and folded across and found tidily laid by in the cupboard of the brown parlor. For this was poor little Miss Nancy's will, in which (struggling with infinite difficulties of spelling and penmanship) she had endeavored to make a disposition of all that she had, as men do before they die.

And so she had devised the best thing she had got to dear daddy, "because of loveing him most;" and Keep Sakes to Aunt Norreys, and the rector, and Trimmer, and Mrs. Plummett, and all the servants. And Miss Nancy wished extremely much that she had some Goods that might have been devised unto God's poor forever, but was "afrade" that she had not got Any Thing. For she had not even got what she wanted to have most of all; but she was trying to have it, and would go on trying more and more, until at last she would be able, even in the things that were hard, to have the thankful heart.

And the rector and the squire sat silent for a long, long time; until the rector rested his face upon his hands, and said in a low voice, "Open our eyes, O Lord, that we may see! Not alone in our joys — even in the things that are hard, give unto us also that thankful heart."

But upstairs the long night went on, and the dreams, too, went on and on; until at last there came one quite different from all the others.

It was a dream of a half-open window, of clouds fleeting over the blue sky, of a soft spring wind, of a sound of lambs bleating faintly on the uplands, of the rooks cawing to each other, of the birds on the elm-tree tops, of a world that was new.

And with that, Miss Nancy awoke; and perceiving that her dreams were over, naturally concluded that the long night was also over, and the morning was come; and looking round with a faint, strange interest, she said feebly, but quite clearly, and with excessive politeness, "Good-morning, Trimmer."

"Good-morning, Miss Nancy," replied Trimmer soberly, it being four o'clock in the afternoon; but quite unaware of any discrepancy, Miss Nancy acknowledged the response with a smile of weak affability. On which poor Trimmer the stern, who had hitherto refused to permit herself to give way for one single moment, went quickly out to call Aunt Norreys, and retiring to Mrs. Plummett's room, sat down on the nearest chair, and went into hysterics.

But Miss Nancy presently fell asleep in much tranquillity, and slept very soundly for a long time; and by and by she had the most singular dream of all. For she dreamed that the squire was in the room, and he was kneeling at the foot of the bed, as if he were saying his prayers, which was surely a very curious thing to fancy in her room. In her dream the door was a little open, and there came a footstep falling softly down the passage, and suddenly the rector was standing outside the door. And then dear daddy rose to his feet and looked at the rector, and the rector tried to speak, and could say nothing, and so dear daddy spoke.

"John Throgmorton desires to give

thanks for great mercies vouchsafed to him." . . .

And so Miss Nancy's waking dream passed into a sleeping, and she thought she was in church, and the rector was praying, and every one was giving thanks with him. And behold, Master Bartlemy was kneeling under the sunny window, with his hands crossed on his breast and his face looking upward; and he prayed, and Miss Nancy heard him.

"And we beseech Thee, give us that due sense of all Thy mercies, that our hearts may be unfeignedly thankful, and we show forth Thy praise, not only with our lips, but in our lives; by giving up ourselves to Thy service, and by walking before Thee in holiness and righteousness all our days; through Jesus Christ our Lord. . . Amen."

IX.

MISS NANCY was convalescent. To be sure she did not quite recover after a few days, as in the old manner of having a sore throat; for she had been so ill on this occasion that it had been confidently believed that she would never have a sore throat again, or indeed pain of any sort whatsoever. She was nursed for a long time; but thinking of what might have been, her friends did not seem to mind the nursing, as she feared now and then they must do. Miss Nancy was herself much affected by everybody's love and care; she could never have supposed that there were so many people to think of her, especially when she put her own qualities under a rigorous examination, and fully acknowledged that she was not as beautiful as mother, not as much to be loved as dear daddy, not as saintly in life as the rector, not as perfect in manners as Aunt Norreys, not as tidy as Trimmer.

But now Miss Nancy was more than convalescent; she was to be considered quite well again. It was a soft, warm day in spring, and Miss Nancy was about to enjoy the air; indeed, to take her first walk beyond the garden. Trimmer had dressed her quite gently; she had not once reproachfully accused her of having grown, — and yet, during her illness, Miss Nancy undoubtedly had done so, — and she had not even told her to mind her behavior. Miss Nancy thought of it afterwards, perceiving an opportunity for taking a little license if she chose, but continued to mind her behavior all the same, because it did not seem quite honorable to do otherwise, when Trimmer had only forgotten to mention it. For this was a very great occasion, one of the greatest in Miss Nancy's life. She was eleven years old to-day, and she was to accompany the squire and the rector on a most solemn and important walk, according to a special request, preferred by her on the excellent grounds of her birthday, and granted on the spot.

They went slowly through the Hall fields, Miss Nancy between her two tall companions, with one thin little hand in the squire's big palm, and the other full of primroses, that the rector plucked from amongst the grass, and gave to her for a birthday nosegay.

So they went through the churchyard,

up the forgotten little lane, and along the pathway in the buttercup meadow to the courtyard of the Thankful Heart. The pigeons fluttered and strutted in the sun, and the water rippled in the basin as of old; but Miss Nancy stood and looked up at the words cut in the oak beam over the doorway:

"In the Yeare of Our Lorde
. . . . . .
"Given unto God's Poore for ever in Token of the Thankful Heart. Amen."

And beneath, another hand had carved new words:

"In the Year of Our Lord
. . . . . .
"John Throgmorton endowed again this House, by the blessing of God, and the Light of a Bright Example, in Token of the Thankful Heart. Amen."

And behold, God's poor were come to their own again, and sat on the benches in the sunlight, and took their rest in the peace of the Thankful Heart. And the shepherd's wife, installed in the great kitchen, stood in the doorway with the children about her. There was Grandfy Purcell, the oldest inhabitant of Forest Morton parish, so old that he had, as he said, "lost count of himself." There was his neighbor, piping his still cheerful note in its shaking treble, "It's old Samu-el; and he's very much obliged to you," while his head nodded and his withered hands shook in rivalry. There was Jonathan, with his dull strain, "I don't hear you. I be stone deaf, I be." There was old Betty, who had outlived her home, her children, and all that she had, and only cared now to gradually sleep herself away, and so sat sleeping on, until she should be rested, and ready to awake at the last. There was witless Mary, who was sixty years old, and yet was treated like a child of six, on account of being quite simple; and yet was not unhappy, because she had never passed beyond the days of her childhood, and in this life never would. There was poor ailing Hannah, who was bowed almost double with rheumatism, and would be straight no more again, until, like the lame man of old, she found herself outside the Beautiful Gate. But until that hour should come, she sat and took her rest, with the others of God's poor, in the peace of the Thankful Heart.

"And may we stay at the church a moment?" asked Miss Nancy, as she went homeward through the meadow, between the squire and the rector. "Because I have been thinking of Master Bartlemy a good deal to-day, and I should like to give him some of my primroses, if I might. For I am so very glad about the Thankful

Heart; I think I feel like he used to do, full of happiness and thankfulness. Do you, daddy?"

The squire did not speak, perhaps he could not; he held Miss Nancy's hand more closely.

"My little maid, we all have thankful hearts this day," said the rector, and there were, though Miss Nancy did not see them, tears in his eyes.

They came to the wicket in the churchyard wall. The birds flew out at their approach, and chattered what was perhaps a welcome to little Miss Nancy; and they went into the low green porch, and through the dark church, to Master Bartlemy's window. The sweet wind from the uplands stole in through the open lattice; and it might have been the spirit of spring bringing Master Bartlemy a message from the old forest, for he lay and smiled in his sleep. And so Miss Nancy was lifted up with her primroses, and left them lying upon Master Bartlemy's bosom, with the sunshine upon him, and upon his noble handiwork round about him: the twelve apostle panels upon the walls, wrought so long ago, and still sound and true as English oak was wont to be, and beautiful with the reverent labor of those cunning artist fingers.

Upon each panel the figure of a holy apostle; and round about him the fret of leaves and flowers, as it were for beauty; and beneath each panel the border of the garbs of a long life, for service; and above, the angel, for praise; and in his hand the palm, for victory; and humbly wrought in a hidden corner, the sign of Master Bartlemy's own hand, the heart, as it were for thanksgiving.

Miss Nancy stood with the squire and

the rector at the door, lingering and looking back.

"I was thinking that if people have forgotten that Master Bartlemy gave the Thankful Heart, they would forget that dear daddy endowed it again, and I was sorry; but when I look at Master Bartlemy, I feel," said Miss Nancy, — "I feel as if it would not matter."

"No, it will not," said the rector, "for the tablet that I think of will keep forever the memory of this John Throgmorton, who by the blessing of God, and the light of a bright example, endowed again the house of the Thankful Heart, for the service of God's poor forever."

"Who by the blessing of God, and the light of a bright example," repeated Miss Nancy, lovingly. "It means dear Master Bartlemy, doesn't it?"

"Not Master Bartlemy alone, my little

maid," said the rector, — "not Master Bartlemy alone."

"The light of all the good people who ever lived?" asked Miss Nancy, wistfully. "Do they all leave a light?"

"There never yet was such a light lost," said the rector. "After so many years — Lord, how wonderful."

"The sun shines so beautifully about Master Bartlemy now," whispered Miss Nancy. "Don't you think it might be like his light shining before men?"

"I think it might, my little maid," said the rector, "shining before men to the glory of God. And if so clearly here upon this earth, how much more, O God, in thy heaven."

And Miss Nancy looked out beyond the churchyard trees, at the blue of the spring sky, and the soft gray of the rolling uplands that had once been Morton Forest, and, beneath the green of the hanging birchwood, the gables of the Thankful Heart, where, in the courtyard, the pigeons came down, and fluttered and strutted for the very joy of life, and the water rippled, "Give thanks, give thanks, give thanks!" And God's poor sat out in the sunlight, waiting awhile, until friend Death should come to ease them of the burden of dulling poverty and long years, in the quiet harbor of the Thankful Heart.

And Miss Nancy looked within again, upon Master Bartlemy, where he lay upon his tomb, and smiled, as one might smile whose name has passed into a better keeping than this of ours. Oh, thou gentle, God-fearing, old craftsman, surely not forgotten, seeing thou wert gone to the place where good men go when they die, to the place where the memory of them abides, and there is no forgetting. Oh, Master

Bartlemy, lying there in ruff and gown, with delicate artist hands crossed peacefully on thy breast; with thy sweet, refined face at rest, and lips parted as if to give thanks now and forever, well, well was it with thee, having brought thy steadfast life to a good ending, — the steadfast life which faithfully serves its generation, and the good ending which leaves behind a light to shine before men, to the everlasting glory of God.

www.ingramcontent.com/pod-product-compliance
Lightning Source LLC
Chambersburg PA
CBHW031452160426
43195CB00010BB/952